For Harry, my original froglet.
— I. M. T.

For Linda, astronaut in pyjamas!
— D. E.

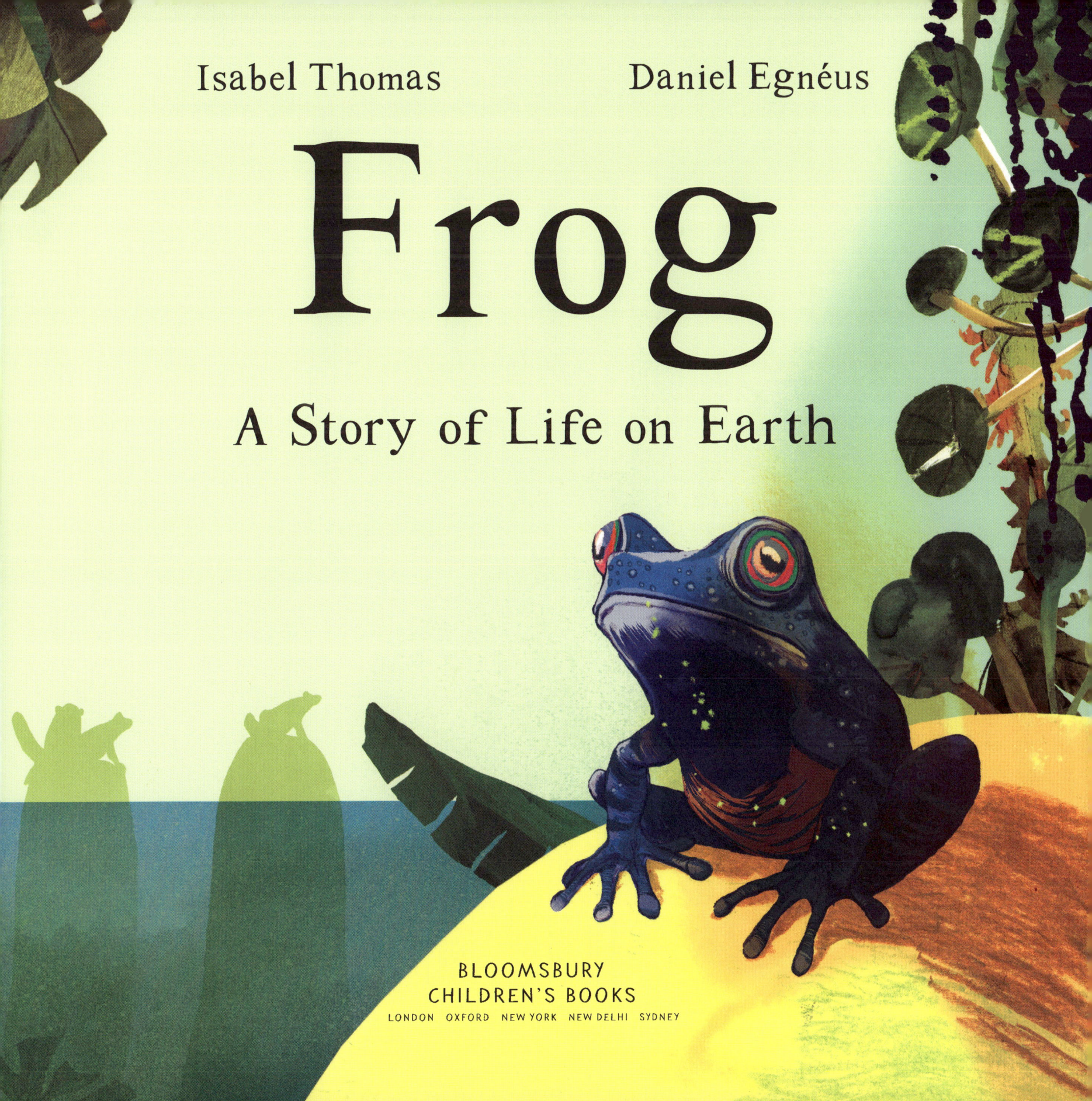

Isabel Thomas   Daniel Egnéus

Frog

A Story of Life on Earth

BLOOMSBURY
CHILDREN'S BOOKS

LONDON   OXFORD   NEW YORK   NEW DELHI   SYDNEY

Look! It's a pond
full of jelly-like eggs

that will one day
be tadpoles,

that will one day grow legs

and will one day be frogs
that lay eggs of their own.

But if frogs
come from eggs,

and eggs come
from frogs,

where did the first
frog come from?

To find out, we must go back
to a time before frogs,
before people and plants,
before Earth and stars . . .

Back to the beginning.

When everything that is, was, and ever will be
was squashed together

in a superheated speck

too tiny to

imagine.

Suddenly, the speck began to expand . . .
. . . and with a **Big Bang** became a universe.

Still small enough to hold in your hands,
the new universe fizzed with energy.

But there were
no frogs yet.

One second later
(the very first second there had ever been)
teeny, tiny specks of stuff began to appear,

dashing and veering,

colliding,

disappearing.

Only when the universe cooled enough
could specks clump together

and form the
very first atoms.

As the universe Kept growing,
gravity gathered atoms in clouds
so HUGE and hot and dense

they collapsed . . .

igniting the very
first stars.

In these fiery furnaces, atoms
smashed together to make
bigger atoms.

Billions of years later,
the largest stars began to

explode,

flinging atoms across the universe.

Stardust is the stuff that forms new stars and planets, moons and mountains, forests . . . and frogs.

But there were no frogs yet.

Eight billion years after the Big Bang,
stardust formed our Sun —
a new star surrounded by swirling dust and gas.

Gravity got to work again,
gathering the gas and dust into eight planets.

Some huge,

some
small,

some
hot,

some cool

and one positioned
best of all.
Earth.

Not too hot, and not too cool,
the surface of Earth was soon
covered in pools of water

which rained
from the sky

and collected in
dips and dents.

All living things need water,
including frogs.

But there were
no frogs yet.

Each shallow pool was just a hot soup of chemicals
reacting, changing, rearranging.

Until one day,
in one pond, something
spectacular happened.

Chemicals, just like any others,
rearranged themselves to form
the mother of every other living thing –

the very first cell.

Unlike stars or sand,
cells can copy themselves . . .

. . . from **one** to **two**,

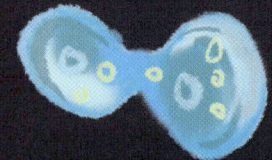

from **two** to **four**,

from **four** to **eight**

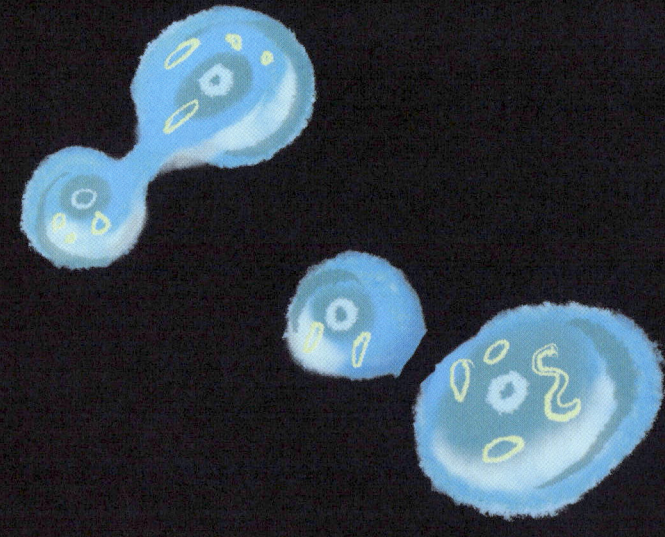

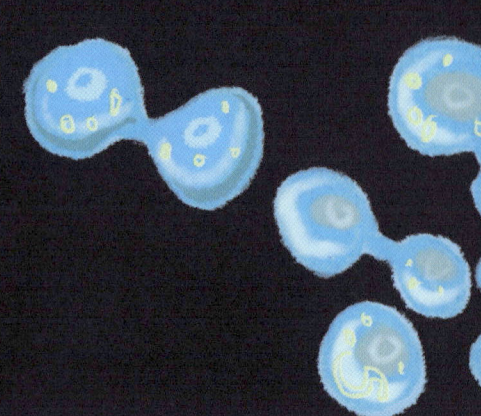

and many more.

Soon Earth's oceans teemed with tiny creatures.

Each one just a single cell,
struggling to survive
long enough to multiply.

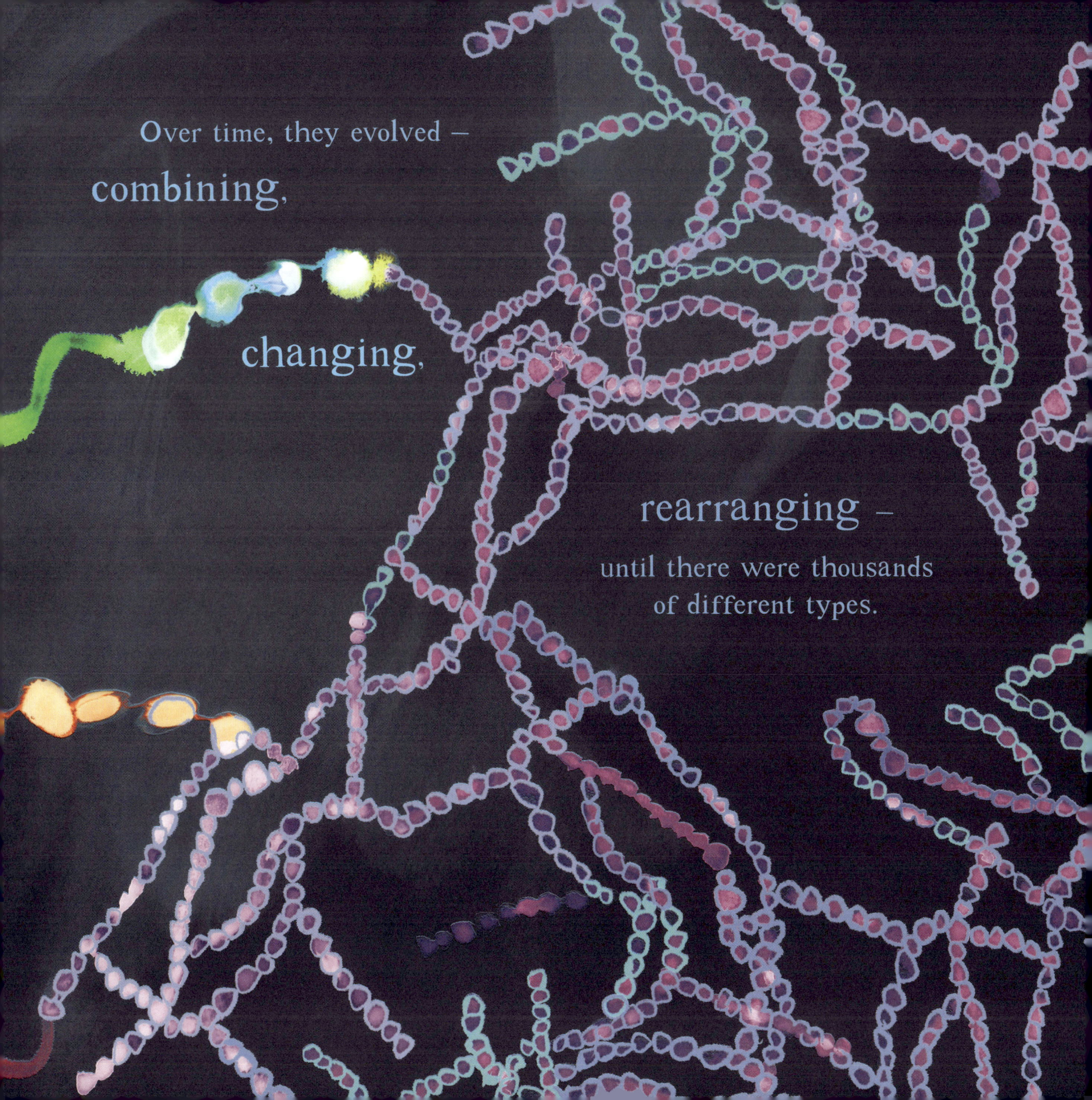

Over time, they evolved –

combining,

changing,

rearranging –

until there were thousands
of different types.

Some cells survived by clumping together to form larger living things.

Frogs are made up of many cells . . .

. . . but there were
no frogs yet.

The first animals were still and silent,
simply sitting in the sea,
sifting food from the water.

But animal life
soon evolved too . . .

. . . from sponges
to sea squirts

to fish that laid eggs.

The seas became so crowded that
life began to move onto land.

Plants and microbes were first to
explore Earth's silty shores,

followed by fish with fleshy fins
that slowly evolved into walking limbs . . .

. . . amphibians!

Amphibians led a double life —
foraging for food on land,

finding water to
lay their soft eggs.

For one hundred million years,
they ruled the land . . .

. . . adapting, changing, rearranging
life on Earth.

Amphibians are the ancestors of
every animal with four limbs,

whether legs,

or flippers,

arms,

or wings,

including . . .

...the very first frog!
An animal that hops ...

. . . and hides,

adapts,

survives.

Long after the dinosaurs died,
frogs still thrive

everywhere water
meets land.

From muddy swamps to tropical trees

to deserts where water
drifts in on the breeze.

Just like their ancestors,
frogs lay eggs

that hatch
into tadpoles,

that will one day grow legs

and will one day
be frogs

that lay eggs
of their own.

Next time you see a
tadpole, egg, or frog,
marvel at this animal
like any other,

formed from stardust scattered through space,
created by chemistry, conditions and chance.

Not just a frog,
but the story of the universe, retold.

The Story of Everything

*If frogs come from eggs, but eggs come from frogs,
then where did the first frog come from?*

To answer this question, scientists seeK clues – in a
frog's life cycle and the building blocks of its body.
In ancient fossils and the light from distant stars.
These clues allow us to looK bacK in time and
find out how life itself began.

The universe begins

By gazing at starlight, cosmic dust and speeding galaxies, scientists have worked
backwards to the moment that space and time began, almost 14 billion years ago.
That moment is Known as the Big Bang.

At first, the universe was unimaginably hot. As space expanded, the universe
cooled. Tiny specKs of matter came together to form the first atoms. Atoms are the
building blocks of every object you can thinK of, from planets to people.

Around 200 million years after the Big Bang, gravity drew clumps of atoms together to
form the first stars. When these stars died, the larger atoms forged inside them were
scattered across space. This stardust became the raw material for new stars.

Our Solar System forms

Our nearest star, the Sun, formed about 9 billion years after the Big Bang.
Leftover gas and dust came together to form the other objects in our Solar System,
including planet Earth.

The young Earth was a hot and hostile place. It was 500 million years before
the planet cooled enough for water to rain from the sKies. As water flowed
across the world's surface, different chemicals were washed into pools.
Mixing in water gave these simple chemicals the chance to linK together
in new combinations, forming new substances. After millions of years
of changing and rearranging, an extraordinary chemical appeared
by chance. A chemical that could copy itself.

The first living things

Around 4 billion years ago, these complex, self-copying chemicals began to build tiny compartments around themselves – the very first cells. Inside each cell, protected from the outside world, chemicals could be rearranged to release energy and reassembled to build useful parts. Cells could grow, get rid of waste, sense the world around them and respond. They could make copies of themselves, passing on the instructions for doing all this to brand new cells. These tiny cells were the first living things.

As cells copied themselves in their trillions, mistakes were sometimes made. Each cell was a little different from the others around it. The cells that, by chance, were best suited to their habitat survived the longest and passed on their features to the next generation. The oceans were soon crowded with tiny living creatures of many different types. As they lived and died, they reshaped Earth's air and water.

The first animals

Some cells began working together, forming larger and more complicated living things. These included the first plants and animals. Like all living things, they competed to survive and multiply, slowly changing as they adapted to their surroundings. Gradually, many new types of animals evolved, including fish that made copies of themselves by laying eggs. Each fertilised egg was a single cell with the instructions to develop into a new fish.

From water to land

Around 400 million years ago, certain fish began spending time out of the water. Fish were not the first living things to move from the seas to the shores. Plants and invertebrates beat them to it. But fish quickly found new ways to survive and thrive on dry land. Over time they evolved into the very first amphibians. This name means 'double life', because ancient amphibians lived on land, but had to return to water to lay their soft eggs.

The first amphibians are the ancestors of every other animal with four limbs, including legs and flippers, arms and wings. These 'tetrapods' include every reptile, bird, mammal and amphibian past and present, from dinosaurs to dogs and flamingos to frogs.

The first frogs

Fossils tell us that the very first frogs lived at least 250 million years ago. Modern frogs are very different from their ancient amphibian ancestors, but they share the same double life – living on land but returning to watery places to lay their eggs. This pattern has been passed on to 8000 types of frogs, toads and other amphibians that hop and slither around our planet today.

The story of life on Earth has been unfolding since the beginning of space and time. It is written into the life cycle of every frog, and it is your story too. You are also formed from stardust and shaped by cosmic chemistry, chance and the conditions on our extraordinary planet.

You are a whisper of the past.

You are a wonder of the universe.

BLOOMSBURY CHILDREN'S BOOKS
Bloomsbury Publishing Plc
50 Bedford Square, London, WC1B 3DP, UK
29 Earlsfort Terrace, Dublin 2, Ireland

BLOOMSBURY, BLOOMSBURY CHILDREN'S BOOKS and the Diana logo
are trademarks of Bloomsbury Publishing Plc

First published in Great Britain 2025 by Bloomsbury Publishing Plc

A catalogue record for this book is available from the British Library

ISBN: 978-1-5266-0075-2
2 4 6 8 10 9 7 5 3

Printed in China at Leo Paper Products, Heshan, Guangdong

To find out more about our authors and books visit www.bloomsbury.com and sign up for our newsletters